Working
at
prayer

To Donald Swann
who has shared so much of my thinking

Working at prayer

by FRANK TOPPING

Illustrations by Noeline Kelly

LUTTERWORTH PRESS
Cambridge

Lutterworth Press
P.O. Box 60
Cambridge CB1 2NT

By the same author: *Lord of Life*
Lord of my Days
Lord of the Evening
Lord of the Morning
Lord of Time
Pause for Thought with Frank Topping
The Words of Christ
Wings of the Morning

British Library Cataloguing in Publication Data available.

Copyright © Frank Topping 1981

First published in 1981 by Lutterworth Press

Reprinted 1982, 1988

ISBN 0-7188-2504-7

Printed in Great Britain by
The Guernsey Press Co. Ltd., Guernsey, Channel Islands.

CONTENTS

Prayer Books and Great Prayers

Epilogue

Looking at Methods

BEING STILL

Over the past few years so many people have written to me asking about prayers and the question of 'how to pray' that I thought I would take the bull by the horns and attempt a practical consideration of prayer. I have no pretentions about being any kind of spiritual authority. I simply hope that my own experiences may be of some help to others struggling along the same path.

I owe a debt of gratitude to many people, ordained and lay, and to a variety of retreat houses and religious orders. However, like most people, my spiritual pilgrimage has had to be made amidst the bustle of modern living. It is often this environment that makes it difficult for us to pray. The spiritual dimension seems to be squeezed out of our lives by the pressures of time-tables, telephones, trains, work and family. There are so many demands on our time that it is not easy to pray with any consistency. It is for these very reasons that I want to explore the possibilities of a prayer-life within the crowded hours of earning a living and raising a family.

There are, of course, as many ways of praying as there are people. There is no one rule or method that would suit everybody. We have to work our way through all kinds of methods until we find some pattern that suits us individually. Then we have to be prepared to adapt again and again. The hard fact is that if we want to find ease in prayer, we have to work at it. We have to find out how to order our thoughts. We have to look at all

things that can help us to pray, like passages from the Old and New Testaments, poetry and hymns. We have to explore the great traditional prayers and look for modern prayers. We have to consider things like the practice of silence and meditation and how to make and pray a prayer list, or even how to pray the news.

One of the first things we have to practice is being still. I wonder if you would like to try being still, just for a moment, now. If you are sitting with your legs cross-ed, uncross them. Open your hands and relax them. Relax your shoulders. If your mind is full of the things that you have to do today, forget them just for a moment. Just close your eyes, take a deep breath, let it out and relax. In your mind say this, 'Lord, here I am in your presence, and nothing else matters but this moment of peace.'

If you have done this once, then do it again. Now you have made a start, you have been still in the presence of God, and you can do this several times a day. It only takes a few seconds to relax, to breathe, to be still and say, 'Lord, here I am.'

If you do this just a few times during the day, then no matter how busy you are, or how hectic your life, you will have had several moments of peace in the presence of God. Being aware of the presence of God is the beginning of prayer.

Lord, help me to be still
In your presence
For at least one moment today,
And in that stillness
Fill me with the peace
Which passes all understanding.

A TIME AND A PLACE TO PRAY

In a busy, working day it is sometimes hard to imagine where or when we might find a suitable opportunity for prayer. I think a good place to start is in bed. Before you make the supreme effort of sliding out of that marvellous cocoon of warmth, try to spend at least a minute in prayer. Do not try to pray for the day ahead, that is too complicated and you stand a good chance of falling asleep again. Keep it simple, thank God for the night that has passed and ask him to help you through the next hour.

The first hour of the day is very important, especially if we have to share it with other people. I believe that there are some people who wake up like larks, fresh and bright. For the rest of us the first hour is a struggle. The brain is not sending or receiving messages properly. This slightly confused state tends to make us feel fragile or even fractious. Pray then, before you rise, that no ill-tempered or tetchy word will pass your lips to start the day badly for you or someone else.

Where and when shall we pray for the day ahead or for a particular concern? I am fortunate in that on my way to work I pass a church which is open and I can slip into a quiet corner for a few minutes. Those few minutes make a great deal of difference to the day.

A church is the obvious place to go, but the church on our doorstep is frequently forgotten, perhaps simply because it is so familiar. If we do not have the opportunity to visit a church, then when and where else can we pray? Buses and trains may not seem ideal places, but you can pray behind your newspaper. I sometimes think that the Tibetan prayer-wheel is not a bad idea, that is, something in your hand or in your pocket that reminds you of prayer whenever you touch it. For some it could be rosary beads, not necessarily to say the rosary, but simply to be reminded of prayer by

their presence; for others it could be a cross or a small prayerbook, something that is easy to carry that will remind us to pray.

One last suggestion which might prove helpful. I have discovered how to cope with the boredom of eating alone. I have tried reading and eating but it doesn't really work, and you end up enjoying neither the book nor the meal. It came to me a long time ago. I was watching a mother spoon-feeding her child. With each proffered spoonful she was saying, 'One for Mummy,' 'One for Daddy,' 'One for Uncle John.' It was a game to help a child eat up the food it needed to grow. Well, I won't draw the parallel any further, but a lonely meal can be transformed into food for thought and prayer.

Heavenly Father
Let me see
The moments I can share,
From my rising to my sleeping,
In the blessing of your presence
Through the mystery of prayer.

ORDERING OUR THOUGHTS

Those of us who find it difficult to pray with any regularity are also inclined to feel guilty when we do pray. We begin to have a guilty feeling that the only time we call on God is when we are feeling desperate. Being anxious or upset does not make praying any easier, because when we are worried we find it more difficult to order our thoughts. Sometimes days go by when we are unable to think about anything other than our anxiety. Our problems keep coming back to us, hanging over us like the sword of Damocles.

Some people have said to me, 'I've got so many problems, I don't know where to begin.' I know the feeling. Let's try to sort out our problems into some kind of order. I think that there are about three main areas of worry,

First, health problems, health of mind and body;

Second, family and personal relationships;

Third, work and money.

Most of our worries will come under one or more of these headings.

The first thing to do is to make a list, either in your head or on paper. When people say to me 'I've got so many problems, I don't know where to begin,' I usually reply, 'Well, tell me about *one* of your problems.' When we have isolated one problem then I can say, 'Now tell me another.' It often turns out that there are only one or two major problems, but in our worried state we keep going over and over them in our minds until we become both worried and confused and our problems seem to have multiplied.

If you make a list, you have begun to reduce your problems, in that you can now see clearly what they are. The next thing to do is to make a list of the things that you can do about them. In this list you might see that you can do one or two things, and you can list them as

Solution A or Solution B. You might, after further thought, decide that Solution A can't be done or wouldn't help much — so that leaves Solution B. You might come to the conclusion that there is *nothing* that can be done, by you anyway. Here is the rule to follow — 'Do all you can, and then leave the rest to God.' It is no use worrying about things that you can do nothing about.

Now take your list and your possible solutions and lay them before God in prayer. First, be grateful for all the blessings you have. If you have a home, family, people to love, a roof over your head, food on your table — thank God for those things. If you like, make a list of all the things you can be grateful for. You will almost certainly find that they outnumber your problems.

Here then is a simple order for prayer,

1. Thank God for all your blessings.

2. If your problems are the result of things that you have done, or in other words, your own fault, then ask for forgiveness, and rest assured that God will forgive you, whatever you have done.

3. Ask God for guidance in your problems and the solutions that you have thought about.

4. Say the Lord's Prayer. It is the prayer that embraces everything.

When you have done this, you will feel the weight slipping off your shoulders.

Dear Lord and Father,
We come to you
Like tearful children.
Wipe away our tears
That we may lift our heads
And see the warmth of your love.

ARROW PRAYERS

I am more and more convinced that prayer is a way of life. It is not so much 'words' as an attitude to living and breathing. It is a state of mind, an awareness of God in all our experiences, good and bad. Of course words help — the words of the saints of every age which have captured the feelings common to us all, our longings, our suffering, our hopes, our joys. We can draw from this great treasury of prayer at special times, in acts of worship, or in those quiet times that we manage to set aside for prayer. In the living of our ordinary, work-a-day lives, however, it is not so easy to call on these prayers for guidance or inner peace. Very often it is because we simply do not have time for that kind of prayer. So what can we do instead?

I think there is great value in what have become known as 'Arrow Prayers'. The idea is that in the time that it takes to release an arrow from a bow, a prayer can be released from our minds: a brief prayer of a single sentence, or even a phrase which momentarily makes us aware of the presence of God. Let me give you some examples. If you are going to a meeting or an interview and there are lots of things on your mind, at some moment before that meeting, perhaps as you turn the handle of the door into the room, say this prayer, 'Lord, be in my mind and on my lips.' Another example — if you are about to make a telephone call, as the number is ringing out, say an arrow prayer for the person you are calling. I don't mean just friends or family, I mean everybody you phone — the butcher, the baker, Ingleby, Groons & Grimble Ltd. Whoever it might be, say a short prayer, 'Lord, be with John . . . Joan . . . Mary.' See a child, bless it. See a worried face, release an arrow. See a happy face, thank God.

This is what I mean by prayer being a way of life. It is a way of thinking about people in the presence of God.

The meeting that is preceded by a short arrow prayer is likely to turn out better than you expected; a conversation can be lifted to a different plane if you offer it to God.

Sometimes we start the day in a rush and maybe we are half-way through the day and the idea of prayer, however brief, has simply not occurred to us. I find that I have, almost by accident, invented signposts to prayer, things that remind me to pray. For me, a great reminder of prayer is the sky. At the start of the day I may have hurried to the station, or caught a bus, or walked down a street, and all I have seen has been trains, buses, traffic and pavements. If I look up and see the sky, I am reminded of prayer. It doesn't matter what kind of sky it is, swirling grey clouds or patches of blue smiling at me. To me the sky is like the Spirit of God, ever present, always moving, and when I look up from traffic and pavements I usually find it difficult not to smile, because somehow the sky tells me that God is with me, watching over me, loving me. On my way to work I may forget to look up, but just before I reach the front doors of the BBC, there is the spire of All Souls Church pointing its finger into the sky, and that is another signpost to prayer. A church, any church, whether you go in it or not, can remind you to say a prayer, even if it is only a phrase, released as quickly as an arrow.

Lord, remind me of your presence
When I wake
When I eat
When I travel
When I work
When I rest.
Lord, this day
Be in my mind and on my lips.

MAKING A PRAYER LIST

I have discussed an approach to ordering our thoughts when we were worried or anxious. Even if we are fortunate enough to have no pressing problems on our minds we still need guidelines for our daily prayer. I used to try to think of each member of my family and mentally go through a list of friends and colleagues. This used to get rather complicated because half-way through my mental list of friends I would suddenly remember a cousin whom I had left out of my family prayers. I also found that my mind was inclined to wander as I tried to recall various people.

There is only one answer to the wandering or perhaps forgetful mind and that is to make a written Prayer List. Once I was priviledged to see a most beautiful Prayer List. It belonged to an elderly lady I used to visit. At first glance it looked like a little photograph album. Each page was covered with small photographs. Sometimes it was a complete picture and sometimes it was a tiny head and shoulders that had been carefully cut from a snapshot. By each picture was a name and sometimes a date. The date was a birthday that she wanted to remember. Then as the book progressed the photographs were replaced by a simple list of names. In the Prayer List Book she had written some of her favourite prayers for easy reference. I remember being very moved by the love and care which she put into the making of her Prayer List. It was a private and beautiful work of art, a little jewel which I am sure was treasured by God himself.

For most of us a notebook would be the easiest thing to use. If you have a diary with pages for names and addresses, or perhaps with 'memo' pages at the back, then your diary could be your Prayer List Book. Using a diary would mean that you always had your prayer list with you.

If your Prayer List is long then divide it into sections, perhaps praying for family and close friends at night and the people you work with in the morning. If you have a very long list you could make it managable by dividing it into sections for each day of the week.

It need not take a long time to pray your Prayer List. You need only bring each person before God by name, perhaps praying particularly for those who are sick or who are going through a difficult time. Remembering people before God may do a number of things for the one who prays. If, like my friend, you write down birthdays, then you are not likely to forget those important dates. In addition you may be prompted to write a letter, or make a telephone call or visit someone on your list.

At the heart of your praying is the thought that through the mystery of prayer, the person you have named might at that moment know the peace of the presence of God.

Father, as I remember those I love in prayer,
Fill them and me with your spirit and your love.

PRAYING THE NEWS

I think that perhaps the most difficult thing to do in prayer is to pray for the world. Pick up any daily newspaper and immediately you have a world-wide range of subjects and people to pray for. But it is extremely difficult to focus prayer even on a single country, let alone the world. The subject is too big for us to give it prayerful and considered thought. What we are thinking is an important part of prayer because as we pray our thoughts are re-shaped. If we are praying for someone it is in the very nature of prayer that our thoughts will be generous, patient, forgiving and loving. There must be careful thought in our minds about the subject of our prayers. So it is not very likely that we can pray with much seriousness a prayer which embraces in a phrase Russia, India and America.

One way of praying for the world is to isolate particular people from the different parts of the world and pray for those people. From your newspaper take the name of a person involved in the news of a particular country and pray, not for the country, but for that person. Instead of praying about the enormous problems of continents, pray for an individual who is living through those problems. In this way the overpowering size of the problems of the world become more managable because rather than praying for 'the world', you are praying for perhaps six or seven people round the world. The pictures in newspapers can be very helpful in our prayers for the world. They can help us to concentrate our thoughts. A picture of politicians or soldiers or the Boat People can become the focal point of our prayers for the world.

When I was at college I used to meet some of my friends each morning in the college chapel just before seven o'clock. On the hour we would switch on a radio and listen to the news. As soon as the news was over we

would switch off the radio and 'Pray the News'. In other words we took the events of the news and particularly the people mentioned and prayed for them.

Of course if you only pray the news, your prayer life could become a little depressing. We found that we had to balance the radio news with news of the good things happening in the world. We learned about the good things from church missionary magazines and religious newspapers.

One thing I have found is that after you have prayed for the people involved in the trouble spots and disaster areas of the world, your own problems do not seem half so grievous.

Lord, let my prayers be not so much for far-away places or distant events, as for my brothers and sisters who suffer and struggle, live and die in the same world, under the same sun and moon and sky that covers me. Father of us all, help us to help each other.

PRAYING FOR YOUR OWN NEEDS

One of the great difficulties in praying for our own needs is that we usually think that we know exactly what our needs are *and* exactly what is required to meet those needs. We are inclined to give our instructions to Almighty God. We say, as it were, 'Here is my problem Lord, and this is what I need to cope with it.' For example, we are going to meet someone that we do not particularly like, so we ask God for strength to deal with this person. The answer might possibly be, 'No, you do not need that kind of strength. You need a generous, forgiving heart that will enable you to love this person.'

If we have already made up our minds about what we need, then it is very difficult to perceive in prayer what God would wish for us. So the first thing we must do when we approach God about our own needs is to try and pray with an open mind. We must not come before God with a shopping list of things that we would like him to do. We must remember the prayer of Jesus, 'Not my will, but thy will be done.' We have to be able to say, 'Lord, I lay this problem, this question, this decision before you. Speak to me. Guide me. Lead me. Father, not my will, but thy will be done.' When we come before God in prayer, we must not only submit our problems, but also be prepared to submit ourselves; be prepared to receive his spirit; be prepared to be changed by his love.

This is not easy to do. We usually say, 'Lord, help me to do *this,*' when we should be praying, 'Lord, show me what I must do.' There is a beautiful prayer in the Methodist covenant service of 1755. It is, amongst other things, a description of the state of mind we should have when we pray for ourselves.

I am no longer my own, but Thine. Put me to what Thou wilt, rank me with whom Thou wilt; put me to doing, put me to suffering, let me be employed for Thee or laid aside for Thee; exalted for Thee or brought low for Thee; let me be full, let me be empty; let me have all things, let me have nothing; I freely and heartily yield all things to Thy pleasure and disposal.

And now, O glorious and blessed God, Father, Son and Holy Spirit, Thou art mine and I am Thine. So be it.

If you can lay your needs before God in this frame of mind, then you will surely know his love and his concern for every aspect of your life, and you will be able to receive his Spirit.

CONSCIENCE AND CONFESSION

The person I most frequently deceive is myself. Even the face I see in a mirror is me in reverse. I rarely see myself as others see me. If I have photographs they are usually of me smiling at the camera. I do not see my face when I am bad-tempered; other people do, but I do not.

The principal difficulty in making our confession to Almighty God is that we are often blind to our own faults. We cannot see ourselves as others see us. For

instance, I might see myself as someone who 'likes to get things right'; perhaps I think of myself as a 'bit of a perfectionist', when others see me as being impatient and conceited. I might hear myself talking modestly about my achievements, whereas to other people it sounds like boasting. I have a natural ability to shut out the things I do not want to see about myself.

If we are to make our confession to God, we must try to examine our consciences as honestly as possible. It is not the big sins that are difficult to confess, or face up to, it is those sins which have become so habitual that they are part of our character. They are so much a part of us that we do not see them as sins any more. I once heard a sermon on the evils of gossip. About an hour after that sermon the group of us who had been to church together began to gossip about an absent friend. When somebody pointed this out, there was an immediate reply, 'Oh we're not gossiping about him, we're just discussing him.' It is so easy to deceive ourselves, to make excuses for our favourite sins.

How can we examine our consciences honestly? Let's try to look back a few hours. We could start with breakfast, and ask ourselves this question, 'Did I say anything this morning that I would not have said if Jesus had been sitting beside me at the table?'

I think that the only way we can come to see ourselves is by looking at him. When we look at the face of love, or contemplate his compassion, or think about his goodness, then our weakness, our selfishness, our lack of love becomes very evident. In the light of Christ's love we see the shadows in ourselves.

Jesus promised forgiveness to those who truly repent, but how do we 'truly repent'? Confessing our sins is the first step. Being sorry is the next step. Last, but not at all least, we have to desire sincerely to stop doing those things that bring sadness into the face of Christ. This is easier said than done. I think one way is to try to be aware of the continuing presence of God. Now that is also easier said than done, but here is a prayer that might help,

If only I knew
How to slow down or stop,
To rest half-way up
And not at the top.
If only I knew
How to make worries cease,
Knew something of healing
And living in peace.

If I could just see
How simply absurd
Is my critical face
And my judgemental word.
If only I could
Live a life that was good;
If only, if only,
If only I could!

I wish that I could
For everyone's sake,
Discover some way
To undo each mistake.
If only I could,
When my mind sees red,
Allow that I should
Be laughing instead.

If only I knew
When I should be meek,
Or when to be bold
Or stand up and speak.
If only I could
Say my prayers as I should.
If only, if only,
If only I could.

May every day
Begin with space,
Enough to see
My saviour's face.

May every hour
Possess within it
The space to live
A prayerful minute.

And may I find,
From night's alarms,
The space between
My saviour's arms.

LIVING THANKFULLY

If we have been out to a meal with friends and we are polite and courteous, we will probably send our friends a 'Thank you' note. If we turn to our friends for help and they give it, naturally we will say, 'Thank you.' When we call on God in a crisis and the crisis passes, or somehow we seem to cope with it, it is quite likely that we will forget about asking for God's help. In fact, we may not remember God again until the next crisis.

The people we love most are usually the people we take for granted. We take for granted the love of our parents, husband, wife, children. They often give most and are thanked least. A 'Thank you' to the cook after a family meal will always be appreciated. We frequently take for granted the love that has gone into the preparation of a meal.

The habit of saying 'grace' is sadly becoming less frequent, or so it seems to me. I find people often say grace if there are children present, but not otherwise. I know people say grace privately, but saying grace as a group does unite those around the table in a special way. Instead of just being a refuelling operation, the meal becomes holy, as every meal should.

The practice of gratitude has its own reward. To live thankfully is to be truly alive. It could mean the difference between drifting aimlessly through our days and savouring and enjoying all that there is to be thankful for. To live gratefully is to be sensitive to beauty and love, to be aware of the riches that surround us.

A smiling face is a gift from God. Acts of kindness, songs and music are blessings. If we do not see them as reasons for thankful living, it is possible that we will not appreciate their value, we will not thoroughly enjoy them, or, in other words, we will not be truly alive.

I have said before that prayer is a way of living, a state of mind that enables us to cope with trials and

difficulties. It is also the state of mind that enables us to appreciate the love of God revealed in the people that God has given us to love. It is seeing everything with the eye of faith. It is being able fully to appreciate laughter, children, beauty, age. Everything is seen with fresh and grateful eyes.

I remember meeting a blind woman. Adele Dafesh, who was the head of a school for the blind in North Africa. She came from a very poor Arab village. She lost her sight as a child and as a result was sent to a special school. Eventually she read for a degree and became a teacher. I remember her telling me that she was grateful for her blindness, because it had opened up a whole new world for her. For Adele Dafesh, living thankfully meant a new vision of herself and the world in which she lived.

Father, thank you for the love I have received, for the vision that gives me strength to cope with problems. Thank you for friends, for family, for beauty, for life itself.

REJOICING!

An element of prayer which is frequently forgotten is rejoicing. We take our troubles to God, we ask for help; we take our regrets to God and ask for forgiveness; but I suspect that few of us rejoice in prayer. Perhaps it's bold of me to say so, but I think that there were times in the past when the church put far too much emphasis on sorrow and repentance and not enough on rejoicing. A few hundred years ago the Puritans thought that it was sinful to laugh. Now you might say, 'Ah well, that was the Puritans, a long time ago.' But that attitude still exists. I remember once singing a song on the radio with Donald Swann. It was a funny song, full of innocent fun — we used silly voices and made funny noises — the idea was simply to make people laugh. After the broadcast lots of people wrote letters of appreciation, many saying how much they enjoyed having a good laugh.

But one letter was from a troubled soul who wrote to ask if I had 'lost my faith'. She could not understand how a man who could broadcast prayers and meditations could also sing funny songs.

If you took the trouble to go through the New Testament and count the number of times we are called to rejoice, and how many times we are called to repent, you would find that we are called to rejoice about twice as many times as we are to repent. Jesus said, 'I am come that your joy may be full.'

The word 'rejoice' means to make glad, to cause delight, to make merry, to find enchantment, to celebrate, to exult, dance, skip, sing! And that element should be present in our prayers. To me, one of the most beautiful passages in the Old Testament is in Job, when God is questioning Job, saying, 'Where were you when I laid the foundations of the earth? When the morning stars sang together and all the sons of God shouted for joy?' We do rejoice at the great moments — a man or woman wins an Olympic Gold Medal — our football team scores a winning goal and we shout for joy. When St. Francis of Assisi dedicated his life to God, his view of the world changed. He talked of Brother Sun and Sister Moon. He found that he could rejoice in the beauty of rivers, trees, animals — the whole of creation.

When we say our prayers, we should remember before God the people and events that fill us with joy — the birth of a child, a young couple being married. It will be different for each of us, but for me, I share breakfast with people I love; I cross the river Thames every day and often see the sun sparkling on the water; I hear the sound of children in a playground, and if I do not shout aloud for joy, then at least in my mind I should let my prayer sing for joy.

Heavenly Father, help us to celebrate, to rejoice in the beauty and love that surrounds us, and to exult in the knowledge of your everlasting love.

LETTERS TO GOD

Sometimes when we are worried or have a lot on our minds, we find ourselves searching for a prayer that will meet our particular situation. Sometimes we start turning through the pages of the Bible with the vague hope of turning up a passage that will speak to our condition, which to me is like using the Bible as a horoscope; it's a form of religious Russian Roulette! It is, I believe, much wiser to have an ordered pattern of Scripture reading. As to finding the right prayer to meet our needs — if none of our prayer books, or none of the traditional prayers that we know seem to embrace our particular state, then we must compose our own prayers. I find that the easiest way of doing this is to write a letter to God.

I remember when I was a theological student, being advised never to post a letter written in anger, though writing such a letter might do us a world of good, so long as we tore it up afterwards. Of course, there is a tremendous freedom in writing a letter which nobody is going to read — we can get a lot off our chests. But whether you post it or not, you cannot keep the thoughts of your heart a secret from God. Rather than write a letter simply to let off steam, I think it is a better exercise to pour out to God exactly how you are feeling.

When you write such a letter, you have complete freedom. You do not have to worry about grammar or syntax or spelling. Simply put down all the things that are on your mind. The first series of meditations that I wrote for the radio came about through writing a letter to the Almighty. I remember arriving home very late one night, knowing that I had to write a script for the morning. I was so tired I did not know where to begin. So, as it was my practice to write a letter to God when I was tired or confused, I began to write not a script but a letter to my heavenly Father telling him how I felt. 'Dear

Lord,' I wrote, 'I'm so tired. Why do I let myself get into these situations? I have known for days that I had to write this script. Why am I such an idiot that I leave everything to the last minute?' By the time I had finished that letter I knew exactly what my script was going to be about. Even as I was writing my letter, God was speaking his reply to my weary brain. I have found in writing letters to God that he always answers — with a reply that arrives a great deal faster than one delivered through the post.

Heavenly Father,
You know the thoughts of our minds
Even before we think them.
Help us to bring before you
All our problems, our questions
And all the decisions we have to make,
So that in laying them before you
We will learn your will for us.

PRAYING TOGETHER

I think the expression I hear most often from people who do not belong to the church is, 'You don't have to go to church to be a Christian.' This is usually followed by something like, 'Anyway a lot of the people I know who do go to church are hypocrites.' This is a basic misconception of what the church is. So many believe that the church should be full of people who *are* good, rather than people who are struggling after goodness. It is as if people imagined the church to be some kind of 'Hotel for the Holy' — whereas, in fact, the church is more like a 'Hospital for Sinners.' Jesus once said that he came like a doctor to the sick, and that if you were totally fit then you did not need a doctor. But he also said, 'Come to me all you who are heavy laden, and I will give you rest.' (Well, we all know the problem and the frustration of trying to persuade someone to see a doctor, if they don't want to go.)

One of the problems of praying is trying to find some system, some pattern that will help us to pray regularly. We know from experience that if we pray only when we feel like it, then our prayer life is likely to be reduced to 'fire engine prayers' — that is, prayers that are only called on in an emergency. It is so easy to lapse into long periods when we never pray. That is why Christians must meet together regularly, to have a mutual appointment with God, at least once a week, whether we feel like it or not. I must admit that there are times when I feel spiritually dry. At times like this I just go through the motions. I carry on with the habit of going to church, of belonging to the family of the church. But during these 'dry' periods, I am supported by the prayers of my fellow Christians in the pews alongside me. The church is the Body of Christ. That is why we cannot be 'Christians on our own.' We need to belong to the Body. When I am weak, the faith and prayers of those round me keep me going. The person who thinks that he needs nobody is a sick man. It is a fact of life we need each other. Our Lord encouraged us to come together when he said, 'Wherever two or three are gathered in my name, there am I in the midst.'

Some people find that they need the mutual support of common prayer more than once a week. That is why most churches have mid-week meetings or house groups where people can meet and talk and pray together. We cannot love people in isolation. We cannot remain in isolation and care for the world. We must come together for our common good. If we regularly gather together in prayer, then on those occasions when we pray alone, we are strengthened by the knowledge that we belong to the family of God.

Lord of life, help me to support my brothers and sisters in the bond of common prayer; keep alive in my mind the knowledge that where two or three gather in your name, you are in their midst.

RETREATS

The idea of going into retreat, which is simply finding a quiet place to think things over, is almost literally as 'old as the hills' — or, if you like, as old as Moses. Moses, you will remember, went up a mountain to talk to God. In a lonely place Jacob wrestled with his concept of God, all night long. In the New Testament, time and time again, Jesus spent whole nights in prayer, usually in the hills. The most famous retreat of all was when Jesus spent forty days and nights in the desert preparing for his ministry. Ever since then, men and women have gone aside to pray — some devoting their whole lives to prayer and meditation. Perhaps it is because of these great examples that ordinary men or women feel that going into retreat is a bit drastic — the sort of thing that you might do only once or twice in years.

Let's go back to my first sentence. The idea of going into retreat is simply finding a quiet place to think things over. Now if you are caught up in the daily business of living, whether it's feeding a child, washing dishes, or driving to work, you might think, 'Chance would be a fine thing.' But a retreat can be as long or as short as you like. A ten minute walk can be a form of retreat. If you are lucky perhaps you can take a walk down a country lane, or perhaps round a nearby park. If you live, as I have for years, in a town or city, then even a walk round the block can do the trick. At work I have often used my lunch break as an opportunity to walk alone. If you can't manage a walk, then the next best place, I think, is in bed. Best of all, if you can get a free day or two, is to go to a place away from it all, like a retreat house or a monastery. Now don't be put off by the thought that this would be too expensive. It isn't. It's probably the cheapest possible form of boarding house, with the advantage usually of a chapel, a garden and your own room. If someone asks you what you

want for your birthday, perhaps you could say, 'I'd like a day at St. Quietude's Retreat House.' If you're going to do this you'll want to know what places to go to. Well, there is a paperback book called *Away from it All* that lists hundreds of retreat houses in England, Scotland and Wales. The book, by Geoffrey Gerard, is published by Lutterworth Press. Or, you can write to The National Retreat Council, 3 Gloucester Avenue, London NW1.

Having found your quiet place to think things over, how do you go about it? Well, at a retreat house you can ask for advice. If you are on your own (perhaps for the next ten minutes), a good way to start is with this prayer, 'Into your hands, O Lord, I commit my spirit.' Don't try to arrange your thoughts into neat arguments, or a list of pleadings. Give the Almighty a chance to speak. 'Here am I, Lord. Speak to me.' Let all your problems drain out of you, and invite the Holy Spirit to enter into your mind and fill your whole being. If you only have ten minutes, then you will probably get no further than this, so simply bring your thoughts together with the Lord's Prayer. If it is at all possible, try to read at least one passage from the Bible: you should have a system for this, like working your way through the psalms or one of the gospels.

Lord, into your hands
I commit my spirit.
Fill me with your peace
So that its light
Will illuminate my path
This day and always.

Aids to Prayer

THE BIBLE

I have been writing about various ways of praying —ways in which we can simply use our own words and thoughts, like being still, making prayer lists, ordering our thoughts and 'arrow' prayers. I want to look now at some of the 'tools' that we can use to help us to pray: prayer books, poetry and the great traditional prayers.

Of all the books that can help us to pray, without doubt the best is the Bible. It is not only full of prayers but is also full of stories and the wisdom of centuries that can speak to us in our particular situation. The story of Abraham and Sarah is a story of faith rewarded. The story of Ruth is a story of love rewarded. Hosea is about love that never gives up, no matter how often it is hurt or let down. The Psalms are a collection of ancient prayers and hymns. The New Testament is full of stories about the love of God, about marriage, work, money, life and death. If you never possessed a prayer book but knew your way round the Bible, you'd never be short of inspiration for prayer. That is why I believe that the best aid to prayer is regular and systematic reading of the Bible. Now you can work out your own system for reading the Bible. Choose a book that you want to read, like the Psalms or Genesis, and work your way through it day by day. Or for a few pence you can buy a lectionary. A lectionary is simply a list of suggested readings for each day of the year.

Even if you do follow a regular pattern of Bible reading, you will find that some passages seem to leap

out at you, almost as if they had been written especially for you, and you will keep coming back to them. I think that the Old Testament book that is turned to most often is the Psalms. If you want to find the Psalms, by the way, just open your Bible more or less in the middle and you'll find you are pretty near. (Actually, they're a little bit to the left of the middle.)

If you were to look at the book of Psalms that Dr. David Livingstone carried with him when he was exploring Africa, you would notice that the most thumb-marked psalm was Psalm 23. These beautiful words have brought comfort and strength to millions of people across thousands of years.

The Lord is my shepherd, I shall not want;
   he makes me lie down in green pastures.
He leads me beside still waters;
   he restores my soul.
He leads me in paths of righteousness
   for his name's sake.

Even though I walk through the valley of the
      shadow of death,
   I fear no evil;
for thou art with me;
   thy rod and thy staff,
   they comfort me.

Thou preparest a table before me
   in the presence of my enemies;
thou anointest my head with oil,
   my cup overflows.
Surely goodness and mercy shall follow me
   all the days of my life;
and I shall dwell in the house of the Lord
   for ever.

THE LORD'S PRAYER

The New Testament records that the followers of Jesus asked him directly, 'Teach us to pray.' There are two accounts of the lesson that Jesus taught: one in the Gospel of Matthew, chapter 6, and the other in Luke, chapter 11. To summarise the passages briefly, Jesus said, 'Pray in secret; don't make a show of your piety. Don't babble out lots and lots of words. Your Father knows what you need before you ask.' Luke's Gospel includes a lovely illustration of how willing God is to hear our prayers. He says, 'Which of you, if your son asked you for bread, would give him a stone? So, if you would give good gifts to your children, how much more will the heavenly Father give to those who ask him?' It also contains the famous passage, 'Ask and it will be given to you; seek and you will find; knock and it will be opened to you.' Both accounts include the teaching of the Lord's Prayer, and each version is slightly different.

The prayer that we say today is a combination of both Matthew and Luke with a traditional prayer added at the end. If we tried to reconstruct the prayer of Jesus, using only what we believe to be the original words of both gospel writers, it might sound like this,

Father, hallowed be your name.
Your kingdom come.
Give us today our daily bread.
Forgive us our sins, as we have forgiven sins
    against us;
And do not put us to the test.

As Jesus taught it, it was a short, simple prayer. The word that Jesus used for 'Father' was the word that children used in those days — 'Abba'. 'Father' is a bit formal. The word Jesus used was much more like

'Papa'. So the prayer starts by praising God, and praying that his kingdom will come. This is followed by a very practical prayer, 'Give us this day our daily bread.' There is nothing more basic than our daily bread. We often talk about earning our daily bread. In America 'bread' is a slang word for money. So when we pray, 'Give us our daily bread,' it can mean many things to the individual who makes the prayer. Then we ask for our sins to be forgiven, and promise to forgive those who have offended us. In Matthew's version, he emphasises how important it is to forgive other people by adding extra verses following the Lord's Prayer.

Finally, the prayer says, 'Don't put us to the test,' or traditionally, 'Lead us not into temptation.' This never meant that our heavenly Father would tempt us to do wrong. It means, 'Don't let me be tested,' or perhaps, 'Don't let me be tested more than I can cope with.' In Matthew there is an extra verse which says, 'Deliver us from evil' which, I suppose, speaks for itself.

The Lord's Prayer is profound and yet simple. It says in a few words everything we could ask for. It prays that God the Father will rule our lives. It asks for the basic necessities of life, for forgiveness of sin, and reminds us to be generously forgiving to others. And finally it asks for peace of mind and conscience. No wonder the Lord's Prayer is also called the Great Prayer.

Father, in heaven,
Hallowed be your name.
Your Kingdom come,
Your will be done
On earth
As it is in heaven.
Give us this day our daily bread,
And forgive us our sins
As we forgive those who sin against us;
And do not put us to the test,
But rescue us from evil. Amen.

THE SERMON ON THE MOUNT

I have written about the Lord's Prayer and the passages in the New Testament in which Jesus taught his disciples how to pray. In the Gospel of Matthew this teaching is given as part of the Sermon on the Mount. If you want to examine your conscience in prayer I can think of no better reading to help you than the Sermon on the Mount. The Sermon takes three short chapters in the Gospel of Matthew — chapters 5, 6 and 7. They are short chapters but they are packed with dynamite. The account of the Sermon ends by saying that the people were astonished.

Well, to read Matthew 5, 6 and 7 today is just as disturbing as it was 2,000 years ago. People are still debating this Sermon. Matthew, chapter 5, begins with the beatitudes — blessed are the poor in spirit, blessed are those who mourn, blessed are the pure in heart, blessed are the peacemakers. As a basis for prayer and meditation, the first 12 verses of Matthew 5 could keep you praying and thinking for a very long time.

The Sermon deals with anger, family disputes, lust, divorce, the taking of oaths. It talks about turning the other cheek, about loving your enemies. It teaches about money, 'Do not lay up for yourselves treasures on earth, where moth and rust consume and thieves break in and steal, but lay up for yourselves treasure in heaven.' It teaches about our everyday anxieties, even our worries about what we shall eat, or what clothes we shall wear. Jesus talks about seeing the speck in someone's eye and not noticing the log in our own eye. He tells us not to judge others — to assess the truth in people not by what they say but by what they do. And it ends with the story of the man who built his house on rock, a house that withstood every storm. And the words of Jesus should be the rock on which we build our lives.

Three short chapters — they will take you about five minutes to read, but a great deal longer to interpret, to pray about and to live by.

There is one verse in the beatitudes that needs a little explanation. I remember it always used to puzzle me. It's the first beatitude, 'Blessed are the poor in spirit.' I used to think, 'What does that mean, "poor in spirit"?' Since then I have discovered that in the Old Testament the word used for 'poor' could also mean 'close to God'. 'In spirit' meant 'willingly', 'voluntarily'. 'Blessed' meant 'happy'. So, 'Blessed are the poor in spirit' could be translated, 'Happy are they who willingly seek closeness to God.'

Heavenly Father,
In places my life is built on sand.
Teach me, help me
To rebuild my life on the rocks of truth and love,
And to seek closeness to you
With a willing heart.

THE LAST SUPPER PRAYERS

On a train journey to London with my daughter, we were discussing prayer when a fellow passenger interrupted us and asked if we would mind if he joined in the discussion. He was a young man not long down from university. He confessed that he was not a believer but was intrigued by the faith of others. He asked, 'What is prayer for?' 'What is the point of prayer?' 'What do you believe you are doing when you pray?' They are very good questions.

For most people prayer is seen superficially and principally as asking for things — asking for help, or for guidance, or for forgiveness or for healing. Sometimes, and more rarely, prayer is a way of expressing gratitude. These ideas of prayer, however, do not probe the real heart and purpose of prayer, which is 'to know God'.

There are a great number of passages in the Bible which help us to understand the nature of God and the nature of prayer. To me one of the most revealing passages is chapter 17 in the Gospel of John. The entire chapter is a prayer — a prayer offered by Jesus at the Last Supper.

The prayer does not ask for *things*, but that we will have knowledge of God, that we might know the love of God. As Jesus says, 'To *know* thee is eternal life.' This is what prayer is about, this is what praying is for; it brings us closer to God. Prayer is the bridge between us and the moment we are living in, and God and eternity. For me prayer intensifies life. An awareness of the presence of God can transform ordinary events into exquisite experience.

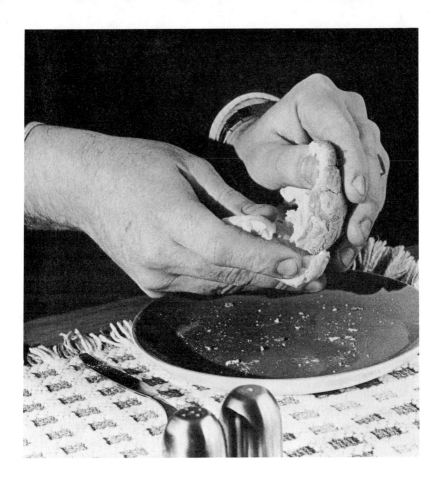

To know thee
Is to be truly alive.
To be one with thee
Through thy Son
Is to be restored to my proper purpose.
To know thy love
In an earthly moment
Is to step into paradise.
Loving Father, look on me
That I might see thy Kingdom without end.

THE PARABLES

One of the best ways of teaching is through a story. Everybody likes a story. When Jesus was teaching, he regularly used stories; roughly a third of the recorded teachings of Jesus are told in the form of stories or parables. Now you might ask, 'How can the parables be an aid to prayer? Were they not used for teaching morals and questions about God and life?'

Well, first of all, as an aid to prayer the parables are guaranteed to set us thinking. The parables in the New Testament are not textbook answers to all our problems. Some of them are not easy to interpret, but all of them make us think. They are stories taken from real life, about real people: farmers, farm labourers, housewives, publicans, merchants, children.

Here is a consideration that is perhaps overlooked. When a story-teller tells a story, perhaps with skill, usually with pleasure, the story and the way it is told also tells us something about the story-teller. Every preacher using an illustration to illuminate a truth puts a great deal of himself into the expression of his illustration; therefore the parables are extremely important to us, because these stories bring us into contact with the mind of Jesus; they tell us a great deal about him. Now if the real purpose of prayer is to know God, then for Christians it is important to know Christ.

In the stories of Jesus we begin to see how he looked at the problems of everyday life, and perhaps we might catch a glimpse of how he, and the Father, looks at us. Perhaps the greatest of all the parables is the story Jesus told of the prodigal son, which tells us that the love of the Father is always waiting for us whenever we turn to him. It is in Luke, chapter 15. This story is sometimes known as 'The Two Sons' — but I would prefer to call it the parable of 'The Loving Father.'

Father,
We thank Thee for Thy Son:
His words reveal forgiveness,
His life the cost of care;
And in His face, Thy love,
Forever waiting
To embrace Thy stumbling children
Who call on Thee in prayer.

PAUL: 'CHRIST IN ME'

In talking about prayer, I have tried to be very practical and down-to-earth; but now, in the words of Paul, 'I tell you a mystery.' I know that some people say, 'Ah, "mystery" — that is the word Christians use when they can't explain something.' Well, I'm afraid that if we are exploring the nature of prayer, we are talking about having a relationship with God. We can *talk* about this, but actually to *do* it takes us into the world of mystery. Mystery is something beyond human reasoning. If we try to achieve union with God through thought, we are involved in what is called mysticism.

Paul talks about living 'in Christ'. For him, being alive meant being in communion with Christ. He said, 'I live, yet not I, but Christ lives in me.' If the object of prayer is to know God, then ultimately we have to invite God to enter into us. No one can explain this personal experience to someone else; just as I cannot taste an apple for you — you have to taste it for yourself. It's a bit like swimming or riding a bike — nobody can do it for you; ultimately you have to launch off on your own, you have to trust that you will not sink or fall. If I attempt to give a child a scientific explanation (even if I could!) of how it is possible not only to balance on about two inches of bicycle tyre but also to travel at speed across the ground, I don't think it would help the child to ride the bike. In the end he has to do it by himself. And if I tell you that you can talk to God, I can't do it for you — you just have to try it. Now supposing you do try it. Does being in communion with God mean the end of all your problems — that you will become a 'good' person? I'm afraid it doesn't. I think that once we become aware of the presence of God we do start a new life — become new people. But we carry on being human beings and making mistakes. The problems of living do not go away, but it is possible to develop an inner strength, an inner core of peace — the peace of God which passes all understanding. Awareness of the presence of God enables us to face life with a new strength.

There is so much in the writings of Paul that can help us to understand the mystery of God living in us. In particular I would like to mention one passage in his Letter to the Philippians, chapter 4, when Paul says, 'Do not worry about anything, but in everything by prayer, let your requests be made known to God. And the peace of God which passes all understanding will keep your hearts and minds in Christ . . . I have learned to be content in any situation . . . In any circumstances . . . I have learned the secret of facing plenty and hunger. I can do all things through him who strengthens me. . . . And my God will supply every need of yours according to his wisdom, in Jesus Christ.'

Lord, help me to enter into the mystery of prayer, that I might live in your love and know your peace.

THE COMMUNION OF SAINTS

In the Apostles' Creed, which is a brief summary of what Christians believe, one of the affirmations is, 'I believe . . . in the Communion of Saints.' What does that mean? Who are the saints?

We are inclined to think of saints as those extraordinary men and women who have been canonised by the Church. But when Paul talked about 'the saints' he was referring to very ordinary people. He used to address his letters, 'to all the saints at Ephesus.' He would send his love to 'all the saints at . . .' wherever he was writing to. To him 'the saints' meant 'those who love God through Christ.' Even today when we know someone who is especially loving and kind we often say of them, 'Oh, he's a saint.'

There are some people, particularly those outside the Catholic Church, who find it hard to accept the idea of asking the saints to pray for them. I think this is because people fear the possibility of idolatry — that is, offering worship to a person other than God. Let's get the whole idea into proportion. If you know that your grandmother is a very loving, kind, prayerful person, and if you had some problem, you probably wouldn't think twice about saying to her, 'Grandma, say a prayer for me.' In this case Grandma is one of 'the saints'. At Holy Communion there is a prayer in which we praise God 'with angels and archangels and all the company of heaven.' The company of heaven includes all those who love God including grandmas, uncles, aunts, cousins, friends, in fact all who share in the love of God through Christ. It also includes those who are part of the 'Church Triumphant' in heaven.

I once heard someone describe his feelings about receiving Holy Communion. He said, 'Everybody receiving Communion is united with me; through sharing the same bread we become one body, united with each other and with Christ. It is as if I was holding hands with my neighbour who was holding hands with all the people who have gathered around the Lord's table right down through the ages, until eventually we are linked with those who sat round the table at the Last Supper, so that ultimately we are holding hands with Christ.' That is a lovely picture of the Communion of Saints. this is why we need never pray alone — there is a Communion of Saints waiting to support us and to join with us as we pray.

Father, when I pray, may I know the joy and support of belonging to the company of heaven through the Communion of Saints.

Prayer Books and Great Prayers

PRAYER BOOKS AND PRAYERS

Near my desk I have a little wooden plaque inscribed with a prayer that was offered by Lord Astley before the battle of Edgehill in the civil war. It is a prayer that can be said before the battle of each new day. It reads,

Lord, Thou knowest that I shall be very busy this day; if I should forget Thee, do not Thou forget me.

Prayers that survive down through the centuries are usually either very simple or very beautiful, or perhaps both. Like the Breton fisherman's prayer,

Dear God, be good to me.
The sea is so wide
And my boat so small.

Or Bishop Lancelot Andrew's prayer before preaching, which is also a good prayer for teachers,

Lord, I open my mouth wide. Do Thou fill it.

I hardly know how to advise about selecting a prayer book. There is such a vast treasury of prayers that have been offered for generations — prayers from people like Thomas a Kempis, (who wrote *The Imitation of Christ*), St. Teresa of Avila, Francis of Assisi, Julian of Norwich and Richard of Chichester. There are also hundreds of modern books of prayers. Visit any good religious bookshop and you will be spoiled for choice*. Have a browse, find a book that will suit you, buy it and keep it by your bedside.

Here is an old and much loved prayer from St. Ignatius Loyola,

Teach us, good Lord, to serve thee as thou deservest;
To give and not to count the cost,
To fight and not to heed the wounds,
To toil and not to seek for rest,
To labour and to ask for no reward
Save that of knowing that we do thy will,
Through Jesus Christ Our Lord.

* Amongst the most well known are Michel Quoist's *Prayers of Life,* William Barclay's *A Plain Man's Book of Prayers,* and *Prayers for the Christian Year,* Bishop George Appleton's *Daily Prayer and Praise,* Rita Snowden's *Prayers for the Family* and *A Woman's Book of Prayers.* There is the Anglican *Book of Common Prayer,*the Catholic missal, and of course the BBC's Daily Service prayer book, *New Every Morning.*

THE PRACTICE
OF THE PRESENCE OF GOD

I have suggested that prayer is not so much a question of words as a way of life; a way of seeing, a way of hearing. A prayerful life is a life that is aware of the presence of God in all things. This is by no means a new idea. In 1666 in Paris, a man who had been a soldier and a servant was admitted as a lay brother into the Order of barefooted Carmelites. He was called Brother Lawrence. For the rest of his life he attempted to live in a permanent state of awareness of God. He was aware that he was attempting the impossible, that he would fail, that his mind would stray away from God. But nevertheless, he went on trying. Now I do not mean that he sat in his cell just thinking about God for the rest of his life. He couldn't do that, because at the friary he was the cook. And the duties of the cook also included buying food and drink for the Order from the French merchants. So he was not cut off from life. As you can imagine, a cook to a very large family is very rarely idle.

There is a little book, about the size of a diary, which consists chiefly of a collection of short letters that Brother Lawrence wrote to a friend. The book is called, *The Practice of the Presence of God*. He said that his work time was no different from his prayer time. He was as much aware of the presence of God in the kitchen as he was in the chapel. He said, '. . . in the noise and clatter of my kitchen, while several persons are calling at the same time for different things, I possess God in as great a tranquility as if I were upon my knees at the Blessed Sacrament.' He said that there was no need to go into a religious order to practise living in the presence of God — it is a question of continuing to do what we commonly do for the sake of God. He does admit that it is not easy. He said that he was troubled with his mind wandering away from God for the first ten years

that he was in the Order. After that he stopped feeling guilty about it and just went on trying.

You can get a copy of the book, *The Practice of the Presence of God,* from any religious bookshop, and as it is only the size of a diary you can carry it easily in a pocket or purse. When I find myself wandering away from an awareness of the presence of God, I frequently turn to the thoughts of Brother Lawrence for help. It is a simple book, but the profound is usually very simple.

Father, this day
Wherever I go,
Whatever I do,
Whoever I meet,
May I travel with you,
Work with you,
Talk with you.
May I live in your love
And know the peace of your presence.

A DAILY OFFICE

When I was a student I went to stay at a Franciscan friary. I was invited to observe the Order at work, or, if I wanted to, I could join in with the friars and follow their way of life. Of course, I said that I would like to join in. I don't think I realised how early they started their day. Every morning at about five, one of the friars knocked on my bedroom door and said, 'Christ be praised,' to which I replied, 'Amen'. This happened every day except Easter Day, when we were woken with a sharp knock on the door and a voice shouting, 'Christ is risen.' And from my slumbers I replied, 'Christ is risen indeed.' Every morning we were in the chapel by five-thirty where we recited various offices until breakfast at eight — and as it was Lent, breakfast was not exactly a feast.

Religious communities follow a pattern of prayer and reading throughout the day. This pattern is called 'Prime and Hours.' This might be allright for monks and nuns, but of course for the average person it would not be practical. But it is possible to follow a simple Daily Office. There are many modern paperback prayer books which provide an uncomplicated system for daily prayer. For instance, there is a Pelican paperback which is called *The Daily Reading,* which can be used with another Pelican paperback called *Daily Prayer. The Daily Reading* is a collection of Bible passages arranged under the days of the week. Each day you can choose a reading and then either say your own prayers or turn to your *Daily Prayer* book. This exercise will take about five minutes or less.

You can also work out your own Daily Office, your own system of prayer and readings. Whatever order you follow or work out for yourself, do try to include a short space for silence — a time when you relax completely and allow the Holy Spirit to speak to you, or perhaps simply bless you with his peace.

I suppose the real difficulty for most people is finding a regular five minute space in which to read or say their Daily Office. Often the first hour of the day is the most hectic and that is actually a very good reason for making time for a five minute space. A prayerful breathing space in this hour calms you down. It can help you to get all your priorities in the right order. Personally I think that it is important to eat first. You need to break your fast. Very often feelings of depression exist simply because we are not meeting our physical needs adequately. It has to be planned. Your five minutes of prayer and reading should become a part of your daily ritual, as important and as necessary as shaving or washing. The peace of mind that is likely to follow does make the effort very worthwhile. It will undoubtedly affect your whole day.

If you find this simply too difficult to arrange the next possibility is probably to use your travelling time to read your Daily Office. On the train or on the bus, instead of reading your newspaper, you might read your Office. Lunchtime is another opportunity. If you eat with others you might have to say, 'I'll catch you up, keep a place for me,' or maybe you can get back to work five minutes earlier. Throughout the day there will be different opportunities for different people and you must do whatever is most convenient for you, but personally I favour saying my Daily Office early in the morning. I am convinced that it is the best way to start the day.

Lord, help me each day of my life
To find time to talk with you,
To hear you in Scripture or in silence
That your peace might be with me
In everything that I say or do.

HYMNS AND POETRY

The poet is constantly searching for the right words to capture the essence or the truth of an experience or an insight. He considers love, life, nature and God and attempts to express his thoughts within the discipline of verse. In doing so he often helps us to gather our thoughts or perhaps introduces us to a new idea. A religious poet frequently intends his poem to be set to music and sung. It is here that the poem and the hymn overlap, but the quiet consideration of either can be an excellent preparation for prayer and meditation.

Here is a verse that is both prayer and poem and is also sung as a hymn. It was written about five hundred years ago and first appeared in print in 1558. Nobody knows who wrote it, but it is recited, sung and prayed to this day.

God be in my hede
And in my understanding,
God be in myne eyes
And in my lookyng,
God be in my mouth
And in my speakyng,
God be in my harte
And in my thinkyng,
God be at myne ende
And at my departing.

For many years I thought of hymns as simply religious songs to sing in church. Of course I realise now that hymnbooks also contain a great deal of poetry — poetry made more memorable because of a tune, such as *Guide me O Thou Great Jehovah* or, *Love Divine all loves Excelling*. Every now and then a popular singer records a hymn which reaches the best-selling charts, like Cat Steven's version of *Morning has Broken* or Judy Collins singing *Amazing Grace*. Then for a short while the poet's prayer is being thought about and sung by thousands of people.

Not many people think of using a hymn book as a book of devotional reading, but there is great spiritual and therapeutic value in simply reading the hymns as prayers. When you look at the sources of many of the great hymns you are sometimes surprised to see that it is a version of a prayer by one of the medieval saints, or perhaps a setting of one of the psalms, or a passage from the New Testament.

There are many poets who specialise in religious verse, from the 16th century poet, John Donne, to more modern poets like Gerard Manley Hopkins and Fred Pratt Green. Many of us will know the songs and hymns of Sydney Carter and Patrick Appleford. Every day it seems there is a new collection of modern hymns and songs, so if you are in a bookshop looking for poetry, don't forget to look in the music and songbook section.

Naturally everyone will have their own favourite poem or hymn, but for me there is a particular hymn which frequently comes into my mind whenever the pressures of everyday living seem to be getting the upper hand. It was written by a 19th century poet, John Greenleaf Whittier. Here are two verses that seem to speak to me,

Dear Lord and Father of mankind,
Forgive our foolish ways!
Re-clothe us in our rightful mind,
In purer lives thy service find.
In deeper reverence praise.

Drop thy still dews of quietness,
Till all our strivings cease;
Take from our souls the strain and stress,
And let our ordered lives confess
The beauty of thy peace.

THE PRAYER OF ST. FRANCIS

I have always found that reading about the lives of great Christians has been a source of inspiration and usually there is a prayer associated with that particular person that survives throughout the generations. I suppose it is not surprising that I have always been interested in St. Francis of Assisi — he is, after all, my namesake. For most people he is remembered as the saint who preached to the flowers and the birds. In paintings he is usually depicted surrounded by the birds of the air. I am afraid that this meek and mild image of Francis does not really do him justice. He was a humorist, a troubadour, a preacher; he was a man of immense strength of mind and spirit. Once he had made up his mind about anything, he would live by that conviction no matter what it cost him, emotionally or physically.

Francis was the wealthy young man who threw his purse to a leper in the days when lepers had to walk about ringing a bell to warn others to keep away. Francis was on horseback at the time. He had thrown his purse to the leper and had ridden on a short way. Suddenly, he stopped, jumped down from his horse, ran to the leper and embraced him: in those days, an unthinkable thing to do.

He had not spent all his life in the pursuit of Christian perfection. As a young man he had been engaged in a local war with a nearby principality, and had spent almost a year of his life as a prisoner of war. On another occasion the romantic Francis had even set out for the Holy Land to join the Crusades. Much later in life, when he did go to the Holy Land, it was as a missionary preacher.

His father was a successful merchant who sold cloth to a variety of royal households. It may have been as a result of his successful business dealings with the French court that he gave his son the French name of

Francis. When Francis decided to dedicate his life to serving God, renouncing his wealth and embracing poverty to live and work with the poor, his father was both incredulous and furious. He thought that Francis was wasting his life. The life that Francis lived, however, has brought hope and joy and love to thousands of people for centuries. Some people believe that his life is the most Christ-like ever lived.

For Francis prayer was a way of life. He saw everything as a gift from God. He saw real wealth in the sky and trees, the moon and sun and stars, and the people that God has given us to love. He saw everything and everybody as his brothers and sisters.

The prayer of St. Francis of Assisi tells us a great deal about Francis. It is also one of the most beautiful prayers of dedication ever written.

O Divine Master,
Grant that I may not so much seek
To be consoled, as to console;
To be understood, as to understand;
To be loved, as to love;
For it is in giving that we receive,
It is in pardoning that we are pardoned,
And it is in dying that we are born
To eternal life.

Lord, make me an instrument of thy peace;
Where there is hatred, let me sow love;
Where there is injury, pardon;
Where there is discord, union;
Where there is doubt, faith;
Where there is despair, hope;
Where there is darkness, light;
Where there is sadness, joy.

THE PRAYER OF ST. RICHARD

In the musical *Godspell* there is a song that is an adaption of a fourteenth century prayer by Richard of Chichester. The song says, 'O Dear Lord, three things I pray: to see thee more clearly, love thee more dearly, follow thee more nearly, day by day.' The original prayer is slightly different. Richard of Chichester started his prayer, not with 'O Dear Lord' but with these words, 'O most merciful Redeemer, friend and brother.' Now that is a very interesting combination of words. Richard looks at Jesus and sees him as Divine, part of the Godhead, the Redeemer, and suddenly the next word is 'friend' — Jesus is not only Divine but also a friend. And then he goes further by saying that he is even *more* than a friend, he is a brother.

The next line of the song says, 'To see thee more clearly.' When Richard wrote his prayer he said, 'To *know* thee more clearly.' I mentioned earlier that the principal object of prayer is 'To know God,' and that is what Richard asks for first, to know him 'more clearly.' We often grow closer to someone as we get to know them, their ways, their likes and dislikes. The more we understand someone, the easier it is to begin to love them, which is what Richard prays for next, 'To love Thee more dearly.' Jesus once said to his followers, 'A new commandment I give you. Love one another as I have loved you, so that all may know that my love is in you.' The way to love God is through loving others. So to love God in heaven more dearly we must look for ways of loving our brothers and sisters on earth. At the time of writing this I cannot get out of my mind the pictures I have seen of the people who are starving in East Africa. Mother Teresa of Calcutta decided to try to do something beautiful for God by loving as many of the poor as she could. Perhaps if I could find a way of helping just one of the hungry in East Africa, that would

be doing 'something beautiful for God.' Perhaps that would be a way of 'loving thee more dearly.'

The last thing that Richard asks is, 'To follow thee more nearly.' This last request is perhaps the hardest of all, because if we follow Jesus closely, if we try to imitate him, we find that he is always giving — giving his time, his care, and ultimately his life for love of us. As a last word, I must warn you that praying is an adventure which ultimately changes us, especially if we do it as the song says, 'Day by Day'.

O most merciful Redeemer,
Friend and brother,
May we know thee more clearly,
Love thee more dearly,
And follow thee more nearly;
For thine own sake.

Epilogue

THY WILL BE DONE

People often talk about the problem of unanswered prayer. I cannot accept the rather facile statement that is frequently offered to those who are worried about this question, that is, 'Prayer is always answered, but God sometimes says "No"'. I believe that every prayer is heard and acted upon. I believe that the question is not, 'Does God answer prayer?' so much as, 'How do we perceive the answers to our prayers?'

The most simplistic view of prayer is that in which it is thought that prayer consists simply of asking for something and getting it. Asking and getting, like, 'Dear God, could you please send me £200 by Monday morning, preferably before 12 o'clock.' If God does not send £200 on Monday morning does that mean that prayer doesn't work? Now I am not saying that the age of miracles has passed, miracles do still happen, but in such a prayer that is what we are asking for, nothing less than a miracle. Miracles do happen. I think one of the most charming stories of 'miracle' that I know was told to me by a Methodist minister who had been a missionary in India. His church happened to be opposite a convent of the Little Sisters of the Poor. He told me that every morning the sisters would go into a field alongside the convent and harness an old horse to an equally old hackney-carriage. They would then drive into Calcutta and call on all the big hotels and restaurants, collecting left-over food. They would then return to the convent and distribute the food to the poor. They had done this for a number of years and the food queue was well known among the poor and hungry of Calcutta.

One morning disaster struck. The nuns had gone down to the field but could see no sign of the horse. They ran to the stable, which was in a corner of the field, to see if the old horse was there. The horse was there, but sadly he had died in the night. The nuns did not know what to do, the food queue was already forming but they had no means of collecting the food to distribute among them. The nuns ran into the convent and fluttered upstairs to their chapel which was in an upper room, and there they prayed, 'Lord, what shall we do? The horse is dead and the poor are waiting for their food. Lord, what can we do?'

Now the field that the nuns used did not belong to them but to a neighbouring Indian Maharaja, a local prince. At the precise moment that the nuns were praying, the prince's chief steward arrived in Calcutta having just returned from England where he had been sent to purchase a particularly fine thoroughbred horse which the prince intended to run in the Calcutta Stakes. The steward put this horse in the field alongside the convent and then went to fetch the prince so that he might inspect his latest acquisition. Meanwhile, the nuns had finished their prayers and were coming down from the chapel. It was then that one of them, looking through a window, saw that there was a new horse in the field. 'Glory be to God,' she cried, 'It's a miracle! Look, God has answered our prayers, there's a horse in the field!'

Without questioning the wondrous ways of the Lord they immediately began to harness the race-horse between the shafts of the old hackney-carriage. Not surprisingly the race-horse did not take too kindly to this treatment and they had a terrible time trying to get him into the harness. Eventually they succeeded, someone opened the gate and in a great cloud of dust they shot off into Calcutta — two nuns hanging on for dear life with wimpoles askew and robes billowing out behind them, people leaping for safety as the snorting animal charged towards the city centre.

A few minutes later the prince and his steward arrived at the field to inspect the new race-horse. Naturally, all they could find was one rather dead work-horse in the stable. The steward was beside himself with horror. 'Has anybody seen a race-horse?' he shouted to by-standers. When told that the nuns had driven off into Calcutta with a rather fine specimen between the shafts, he immediately ran to the prince shouting, 'The nuns! The nuns have stolen the horse!' Now although the prince was not a Christian, he was well aware that the nuns were not likely to take to horse stealing in order to supplement their charitable works. The prince left a message that he wanted to see the nuns on their return. When the nuns did return, they were exhaust-ed. Whilst being very grateful to the Almighty for pro-viding them with a horse, did it have to be this wild, snorting animal? Later they told their story of simple faith to the prince. The horse, although having under-gone somewhat unusual exercise, was in no way damaged or strained. The prince then told his steward to take the nuns to his stables, where he had literally hundreds of horses, and to choose a good, strong, docile horse and give it to the nuns. Being charmed by the nuns' story, the prince made them promise that in future they would come directly to him should they ever have similar problems.

That story is the story of a miracle. First there was no horse, then a horse appeared at just the right moment and finally the problem was completely solved by the prince's gift and promise of future help. The nuns asked and they were given. But that is not the only form of prayer nor is it the only way in which prayer is answered. Let us consider other ways in which prayer is answered.

Sometimes we take our problems to God and the

answer does not involve a miracle. As we pour out our problems it becomes clear that we do not require a miracle to change the situation for us, but that in fact we can change the situation for ourselves. In other words God's answer to our prayers is, 'In this situation I have already given you the strength, the talents, the ability to cope with your problems. I will not change the situation for you but I will show you how to change the situation for yourself.'

The best example I know to illustrate this answer to prayer is the story of two Scottish preachers who every year used to go together on a fishing holiday with their wives. On one particular day they had hired the services of an inshore fisherman to take them out for a little deep-sea fishing off the west coast of Scoltand. Now the two preachers were physically very different. One was extremely tall and broad whilst the other was quite short and thin. They were rather like an ecclesiastical Laurel and Hardy to look at. They were a mile or two off the coast when the boatman saw the first signs of a particularly nasty looking squall. Immediately he told the party that they would have to beat for the shore. He then caused great consternation by muttering, 'We'll not make it though.' 'What do you mean, "we won't make it"?' they asked. 'I mean we will not make it to the shore before that . . .' he indicated the brooding clouds behind them, '. . . before that catches up with us.' At this, the little preacher turned to the ladies in the boat and said, 'Ladies, shall we ask Dougal to lead us in prayer?' (Dougal being the tall and broad man.) The ladies thought that this was a very good idea, but not the boatman. His voice cried out in horror from the stern of the boat, 'Och! No! Away with you! Let the wee manie pray, and let the big one tac' an oar!'

Sometimes God does say very clearly, 'Help yourself.' Or in other words, God sometimes answers our prayers by saying, 'I have given you strength, the talents, the ability to cope with this situation. Use the gifts that I have given you.'

So, prayer could possibly be answered with a miracle that would dramatically change the situation for us, or prayer could be answered, not with a miracle, but by being shown how we can change the situation for ourselves. There is yet another way in which prayer can be answered, but it is a way which some of us find very difficult to accept. Sometimes, God does not change the situation with a miracle, or show us how to change the situation. Instead, the situation stays exactly as it is and God offers to change us.

In the Garden of Gethsemane, do you remember the prayer that Jesus prayed? 'Father, if there is *any* other way, remove this cup, yet, not my will be done, but thine.' Jesus, the Son of God, prayed that there might be another way, but what was the answer to his prayer? God did not provide him with a miracle, nor did he show Jesus how to use his gifts to avoid the suffering that lay ahead of him. Jesus had to go through his passion but he did it filled with the power that ultimately conquered death itself. At some stage in our lives it is possible that we will be confronted with a problem so great that we might pray, 'Father, if there is any other way, remove this cup.' We might want to find a way round our problem, or better still, find some miraculous way of removing the problem completely. At such a time, it might be that the answer to our prayer is that God will offer us something that will change us completely, if we can accept it. I mean that he will offer us the strength that took Christ through the crucifixion.

I remember once, just after I had left my theological college, visiting a lady in hospital. She had been in hospital for a very long time. She was paralysed from the neck down. Every four hours a plaster cast was placed over her. If she was lying on her front there was a cast that fitted over her back. This was strapped on to her and she would be turned over. Four hours later a cast would be fitted on to her front and she would be turned over again. This happened every four hours, day in and day out, week in and week out, month in and month out. Now, imagine that you are a young minister visiting this lady, what do you say to her? I remember thinking that all the normal things would be inadequate. I could hardly say to her, 'How are you?' or, 'How are you getting along?' As it turned out I need not have worried. Instead of my comforting her, she comforted me. She was so full of joy. She was full of conversation and laughter. She read a great deal with a book propped up in such a way that she could turn the pages with a stick between her teeth. The extraordinary thing was that she was so full of life. I came away from visiting her feeling buoyant, uplifted. I began to realise that I had been in the presence of something strange and mysterious and wonderful. In fact I had been in the presence of the power that had taken Christ through the crucifixion.

I believe that there is no such thing as 'unanswered prayer'. I believe that all our prayers are heard and answered. We might receive a miracle, we might be shown how to cope with situations by using the gifts that God has given us, or ultimately, if we are able to trust in the love of God completely, he will so fill us with his grace that we will be able to face anything, even death itself.

So, in the words of Paul, 'Be not anxious about anything, but in all things, let God know of your needs through prayer with thanksgiving. And the peace of God which passes all understanding will watch over you.'